D1395048

20th Century Inventions

FILM AND TELEVISION

Louise Wordsworth

WAYLAND

20th Century Inventions

AIRCRAFT

CARS

COMPUTERS

DIGITAL REVOLUTION

FILM AND TELEVISION

THE INTERNET

LASERS

MEDICAL ADVANCES

NUCLEAR POWER

ROCKETS AND SPACECRAFT

SATELLITES

TELECOMMUNICATIONS

Front cover and title page: A mixing desk in a television editing suite.
Back cover and contents page: A television camera films a tennis match.

Series editors: Philippa Smith and Sarah Doughty
Book editor: Alison Cooper
Series designer: Tim Mayer
Book designer: Malcolm Walker of Kudos Design
Cover designer: Dennis Day

First published in 1998 by Wayland Publishers Limited,
61 Western Road, Hove, East Sussex BN3 1JD, England

Find Wayland on the Internet at http://www.wayland.co.uk

British Library Cataloguing in Publication Data
Wordsworth, Louise
    Film and television. – (20th century inventions)
    1. Television – Juvenile literature 2. Motion pictures – Juvenile literature
    3. Telecommunications – Juvenile literature
    I. Title
    384.5'5

ISBN 0 7502 2099 6

Typeset by Malcolm Walker
Printed and bound in Italy by G. Canale & C.S.p.A., Turin

Picture acknowledgements
Mary Evans 6; Eye Ubiquitous 41/David Cummings; Getty Images 13; Ronald Grant Archive 16/David James, 18/Richard Foreman, 19/Richard Foreman, 28, 29/Frank Masi, 30/Walt Disney Co, 31, 33; Image Bank 5/David W. Hamilton; NMPFT/Science & Society Picture Library 7, 9, 10, 14, 44 (right); Pictor 40; Science Photo Library *cover & title page*/ Phil Jude, *back cover & contents page*/Philippe Plailly, 8, 22 (top)/James Stevenson, 22 (lower)/Adam Hart-Davies, 24/Adam Hart-Davies, 32/Philippe Plailly, 36/Geoff Tompkinson, 37 (lower)/David Parker, 42/James King-Holmes & W Industries, 43/Will & Demi McIntyre, 44 (left); Sony 39; Topham 15, 45 (top); Wayland Picture Library 4/Rupert Horrox, 11/Rupert Horrox, 21/Rupert Horrox, 27 (lower)/Zak Waters, 34/Zak Waters, 35/Zak Waters, 45 (right)/Rupert Horrox; Zefa 22/ J. Maher, 27(top)/Damm, 37 (top). Artwork is by Tim Benké.

20th Century Inventions
CONTENTS

MOVING PICTURES

Film and television have an amazing impact on our daily lives, yet film has been available for only a century, and television is an even more recent invention. Many technological advances have taken place since an audience first sat down to watch a moving picture, but throughout the years film and television have never failed to fascinate people all over the world.

More than 500 million households in the world have at least one television set, while over 300 million households have two or more. Children in the USA and UK spend an average of three to four hours a day watching television. A blockbuster movie can attract approximately 15 per cent of the population to the cinema. Looking at these figures, could you imagine life without cinema and television? How would people spend their spare time?

Teenagers all over the world enjoy a visit to the cinema.

Some people argue that we have come to rely on film and television too much, and point out that there are better ways of spending our free time. This may be true, but it could also be argued that film and television provide us with a great deal of information and enjoyment.

Today, we take films and television programmes for granted. Yet we probably understand little of how the special effects, colour, sound and other features are created and put together. This book will look at the story of film and television, and at how they have developed into the twentieth century's most popular forms of entertainment.

Television is the world's most popular form of entertainment – and can be enjoyed by the whole family.

The first cinemas

The very first films were shown in theatres, shops, or even tents. But by the early twentieth century, the demand to watch 'moving pictures' was so great that special buildings had to be constructed in which to show them. In 1905, cinemas called 'Nickelodeons' opened in the USA. From 1907, British audiences sat down to watch films in 'Electric Palaces'.

THE STORY OF CINEMA

A magic lantern show from the 1880s. Shows like these had thrilled audiences for more than two centuries.

The development of cinema can be traced back many centuries to the time of the ancient Greeks. They experimented with moving shadows, using lamps to make shadows on walls. Shadow puppets were developed, and they have been used to entertain people for hundreds of years. Then, in the 1660s, magic lanterns were introduced. These consisted of a lamp with a candle and a lens, which could project pictures on to a wall. For many years, magic lanterns amazed audiences with pictures of characters from popular stories.

In the 1830s, toys that showed viewers sequences of still pictures in rapid succession were invented. The zoetrope, for example, consisted of a strip of paper with a series of small pictures on it, which was attached to a slotted drum. When the viewer spun the drum and looked through the slots, the pictures appeared to move.

Optical illusions

All moving pictures are really optical illusions, which rely on the fact that the human brain retains an image for a fraction longer than it exists in reality. This means that if pictures are shown quickly enough one after the other, the brain is 'tricked' into seeing a single unbroken movement. This is known as the 'persistence of vision' theory.

Below **Each of these pictures is slightly different. When shown in rapid succession, they blend together, and the man appears to be walking.**

Capturing movement

New inventions in photography were also important in the development of cinema. In 1889, a US inventor called George Eastman developed the first roll of film made of celluloid, a transparent plastic. The glass and metal plates used by early photographers had to be replaced after each picture was taken, but with celluloid one picture could be taken straight after another. It was perfect for recording moving images.

A few years later, a Scotsman called William Dickson invented the Kinetoscope. This projected perforated celluloid film at the rate of forty pictures per second – and the pictures appeared to move. However, they could be viewed by only one person at a time.

The Kinetoscope was the first machine to show 'moving' pictures. Viewers peered down the eyepiece at the top to watch a 'show' that lasted up to twenty seconds.

New developments

The Cinematographe allowed films to be shown to an audience for the first time.

Once inventors had discovered how to make pictures appear to move, they still had to find a way to project the pictures on to a screen, so that an audience could watch them. The problem was solved by the Lumière brothers in France in 1895. They developed a machine called the Cinematographe, which could record moving images and project them on to a screen.

People were soon forming huge queues to see the Cinematographe in action. The films that were shown were very short, and featured events that today we would find rather boring – a baby being fed, for example. But the audiences of the time found them magical and amazing. An audience being shown a film of a train moving forwards found it so realistic that they fled in terror!

Telling tales

Georges Méliès was the first person to show that film could be used to tell stories. From 1896, he based his films on fairy tales and science-fiction stories. They looked beautiful and included special effects to astonish the audiences.

The 'talkies'

The early full-length films had no soundtrack, although a piano or organ was sometimes used to provide music while the film was being shown. In 1927, the first 'talkie' was released. Sound recorded on discs was played at the same time as the moving pictures. For the first time, sound effects and the actors' voices could be heard.

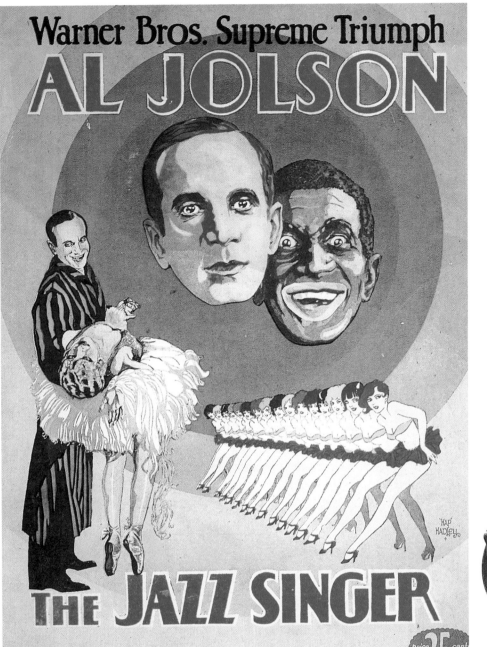

Left **The first 'talkie' was *The Jazz Singer*, starring Al Jolson. It was a great success.**

Below **The Technicolor three-colour camera used red, green and blue filters to record colours.**

Technicolor

In the early days of cinema, only black-and-white films were shown. Colour film could only be produced by colouring in each frame by hand – a time-consuming process when you consider that there are twenty-four frames per second. The Technicolor process used a special camera, which photographed on to three strips of film instead of one. Each strip was sensitive to red, green or blue, and by combining these colours, the full range of colours could be made. By the 1950s, most films were made in colour.

The cinema experience

In the 1930s, audiences queued around the block to take part in the cinema experience. Here, people are waiting to see the Swedish star Greta Garbo in the film *Queen Christina*.

The US film industry began when the first studios were built in Hollywood, a small village in California, in 1910. By the 1920s, more than 800 films were being made in Hollywood every year and it had become the film capital of the world.

Cinema-going reached its peak during the 1930s and 1940s, when many people went to the 'flicks' at least once a week. In those days, a visit to the movies involved more than just watching a film. Cinemas had restaurants, cafés and even art galleries attached to them. Movie-goers would be greeted at the cinema door by a commissionaire in full uniform. An usherette would show them to their seats. While they were waiting for the movie to begin, an organist would play. As well as being shown the main movie, they would also watch a 'B' movie – usually a thriller lasting about an hour – and a newsreel.

Fighting for survival

By the 1950s, cinema was losing its appeal. Cinema buildings were in need of repair. Ticket prices were rising. Television, which had been invented in the 1920s, was becoming more widely available, and it allowed people to watch 'moving pictures' in the comfort of their own homes.

Cinema tried to fight back with a range of unusual inventions that could not be copied on television. These included 3–D: audiences could wear special cardboard glasses with different-coloured lenses that appeared to make the images on screen come right up to them. Another new technique, Smell-O-Vision, speaks for itself. Yet the number of people visiting the cinema continued to decline.

The new cinemas

In the late 1980s, the situation began to improve. The spread of multiplex cinemas was partly responsible for this. Multiplexes are huge buildings that contain lots of separate cinema screens. The biggest in the world is in Belgium and it has twenty-four screens. Multiplexes are usually built on the outskirts of cities, with large car parks and restaurants nearby. As in the 1930s, a visit to the movies now offers all-round entertainment. The film industry is booming once more.

THE TELEVISION AGE

Television broadcasting developed from two important inventions. The first was cinema photography (see pages 6–8). The second was radio broadcasting: the technique of sending sound through the air using radio waves.

Radio broadcasting

Radio broadcasting had been achieved for the first time in 1896, by the Italian scientist Guglielmo Marconi. He had worked out how to use radio waves to send messages over a long distance. Once this breakthrough had been made, other scientists went on to discover how to capture pictures electronically and transmit these by radio wave, too.

Radio waves

Radio waves are invisible ripples of electric and magnetic force which travel through space at an incredible speed (a radio wave can go around the world seven times a second). They are just one of the many kinds of wave that make up the electromagnetic spectrum. Microwaves are also part of the electromagnetic spectrum, and they are used to send signals to and from communications satellites.

Radio waves look like the ripples in a rope when it is shaken. The distance between the top of each wave is called the wavelength.

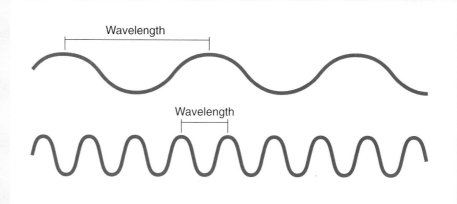

The number of waves that pass a fixed point in one second is called the frequency. In the diagram above, the lower wave has a shorter wavelength and a higher frequency than the upper one. Each radio station and television channel uses a different wavelength and frequency so that the signals do not get mixed up.

The invention of television

The first television set was developed in 1925 by a Scottish inventor called John Logie Baird. In the following year, he showed his television system to an audience and transmitted fuzzy images of a dummy. Other inventors, including Marconi, were also developing television equipment.

By 1929, only 100 people in the UK owned a television set, as they were still very expensive. But the number steadily increased, especially when model kits were developed so that people could make their own sets. At that time, television sets were about the size of a modern portable television. The screen was much smaller than it is on modern televisions, and the reception was not as good as it is today. However, the fact that people could now receive moving images in their homes was amazing in itself.

History in the making: John Logie Baird demonstrates the world's first television system.

Developments in television

The British Broadcasting Corporation (BBC) was the world's first television station. It began transmitting programmes in 1932, but closed down just a few years later when the Second World War broke out. The USA did not start transmitting programmes until 1939 – but one year later there were twenty-three television channels on the air. The first programmes were shown only in the early evening, and there were breaks between each programme when nothing was shown at all. The programmes included plays, news, sports and children's programmes.

When the Second World War was over, the BBC began showing television programmes again. In 1953, sales and rentals of television sets increased dramatically, because everyone wanted to be able to watch the coronation of Queen Elizabeth II. By 1957, half the British adult population was watching television.

Behind the scenes: cameramen film a television programme in the 1950s.

By the 1960s, many families owned colour televisions. Eating habits changed, as people began to enjoy 'TV dinners' in front of the set.

Bringing colour into our lives

In 1954, the USA became the first country to show television programmes in colour, although colour television was not widely available until the 1960s. Colour television works in the same way as black-and-white television. A television picture is made up of tiny dots. In colour television, the dots are red, green and blue, instead of black and white. Different combinations of red, green and blue dots produce the full range of colours when they are mixed together.

Video-recording

When people video a programme at home, their video-recorder picks up signals directly from their television aerial, satellite dish or cable link and transfers them to the tape. Videotape is different from film: it is a magnetic tape, like those used to make sound recordings. The very first video system was invented by Logie Baird in the 1920s. It was developed further in 1956 and used by television companies to store programmes before they were broadcast. Video-recorders were not generally available to viewers at home until the 1980s.

MAKING A FILM

Film-making today is a multi-million-pound business, and people all over the world enjoy being entertained at the cinema. Hollywood, in the USA, is still the centre for making blockbuster movies, but film-making is also an important industry in many other countries. 'Bollywood', the film-making centre in India, produces more films each year than Hollywood.

Film equipment

Although film-making has changed a great deal since the early days of cinema, the basic requirements – equipment to record the pictures and sound, and to project the film for an audience – are just the same.

The film itself is made from a strip of photographic plastic called celluloid. The holes at the side of the film fit on to sprockets – toothed wheels on the movie camera and the projector – so that the film can run smoothly.

A modern movie camera. The cameras used today look very different from those used by the first film-makers, but the basic process of recording moving pictures remains the same.

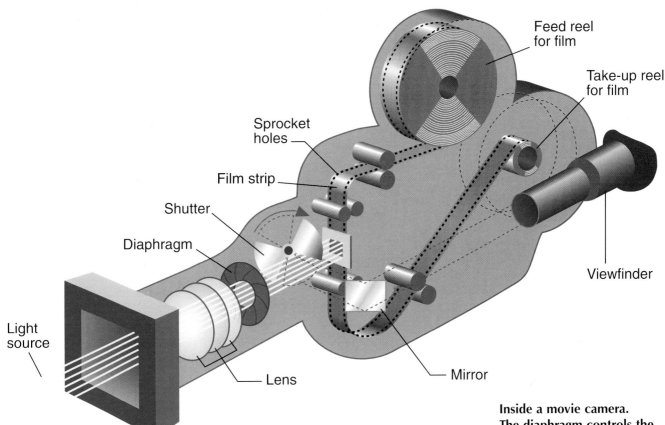

Feed reel
for film

Take-up reel
for film

Sprocket
holes

Film strip

Shutter

Diaphragm

Viewfinder

Light
source

Lens

Mirror

Inside a movie camera.
The diaphragm controls the
amount of light that reaches the
film while the shutter is open.
The mirror reflects light on to
the viewfinder.

How does the movie camera work?

A sprocket inside the camera holds the strip of film and pulls it through the camera so that each frame stops exactly behind the lens. When the frame is in position, a shutter moves out of the way to let light reach the lens and film. A photograph is taken of the scene that the camera can 'see'. Once the photograph has been taken, the shutter drops back into place. This stops any more light hitting the strip until the next frame moves behind the lens. Today, most movie cameras take twenty-four pictures like this every second.

Recording the sound

The sound for the movie is recorded using a microphone on a long arm, known as a 'boom'. The boom operator has to make sure that the microphone does not appear in the area that the camera is filming. The sound is recorded on to a tape machine. This is electronically controlled to ensure that the sound is in time with the action being filmed by the camera.

Behind the scenes

Making a big-budget film requires a large number of people. As well as the actors, there are many people involved behind the scenes, whose work is needed to make the film a success.

The producer is in overall charge of the film from start to finish. He or she has to find a suitable script, hire the staff, obtain the money needed to make the film, and make sure everything runs on schedule.

Creating a 'look'

The production designer is in charge of the overall 'look' of the film, and has to organize the design and building of the sets. The location manager looks for suitable places to film scenes which need to be shot outside the studio. If a castle is needed for a scene, for example, the location manager looks at various castles and takes photographs to show to the director. Together, they agree on the most suitable location.

Hours of careful preparation are needed to create scenes that look dangerous and exciting on the screen. The set has to be safe for the actors and film crew to work on.

Filming a scene from *Speed*. The clapperboard is held in front of the camera to mark the beginning of each take.

Shooting the scenes

The director is in charge of filming. He or she makes decisions about how each scene should look and how the actors should deliver their lines. The director of photography works with the director, deciding on the camera angles, the lenses to be used and the lighting, to ensure that the pictures the audience sees on the screen look perfect. The camera operator makes sure that each scene is in frame and in focus.

The clapperloader works as the camera operator's assistant, loading the film into the camera and sending it to be developed at the end of each day's filming. The clapperloader also writes the scene number and the take on the clapperboard at the beginning of each take, and claps the clapperboard in front of the camera. This is so that each shot can be put together in the right order by the film editor.

Editing

Each scene is shot many times and from different angles. The film editor works with the director to put together the best takes to create the story of the film. The director looks at each take and decides which ones work best. The selected shots are then put together by the film editor.

Projecting a film

The projection room in the cinema is the control centre for everything that goes on in the auditorium. From here, the lights are dimmed, the music is played while the audience waits for the film to start, and the curtains are drawn. Most importantly, the film is projected from this room, through a small window at the back of the auditorium.

The projectors

The reels of film arrive in tins. Each reel lasts for about twenty minutes, so an average film lasting ninety minutes will use five reels.

Inside a film projector. Light from the powerful lamp inside the projector is directed on to the film strip by the condenser lenses.

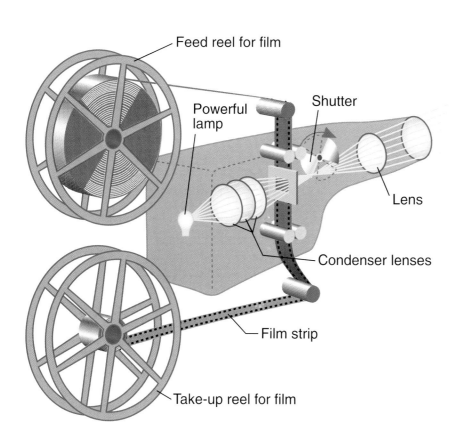

Feed reel for film

Powerful lamp

Shutter

Lens

Condenser lenses

Film strip

Take-up reel for film

A reel of film is placed in the projector spoolbox. The sprocket holes along the edges of the reel are held by the claws of the roller, in the same way as they are in the camera (see page 17). Like the camera, the projector pulls the film through at regular intervals. The difference is that when the shutter moves out of the way of the lens, a light inside the projector shines on to the frame that is in position. The picture that is on the frame is magnified and projected on to the screen in the auditorium. The shutter then covers the lens while a new frame slides into place. The images overlap at the rate of twenty-four frames per second to give the impression of a moving picture.

Picking up the sound

Each frame continues to the soundtrack reader. Here, a light shines through another lens (the optical head-reader) and on to a band on the side of the frame that carries the soundtrack. The information from the soundtrack is picked up and carried to a photoelectric cell which beams the sound to the loudspeakers in the auditorium.

The film then moves on to the take-up reel where it ends its journey. This process is repeated for each reel of film.

The reels of film are fed through the projector by the projectionist. The film is projected on to the cinema screen through the small square 'window' in front of the projector.

TELEVISION PROGRAMMES

In the control room, the director watches rows of screens. These display the shots taken by the cameras in the studio.

Most television programmes are made in a studio, and a television station usually contains several different sizes of studio. The studios contain the sets needed for the programmes, with the background and props needed for each scene.

Television cameras

The television cameras are positioned in the studio. More than one camera is used, to shoot the scene from different positions. These shots are mixed together, so that the viewer does not see the scene from just one angle. Television cameras work differently from film cameras because they do not carry film or videotape. Instead, they turn light into electric currents, or 'picture signals'. These are sent down a cable and either broadcast straightaway ('live'), or recorded on to videotape, so that they can be stored and transmitted later.

The production control room

The images from the cameras are displayed on screens in the production control room, where the director sits. He or she uses a microphone link to give instructions to the crew in the studio. They pick up the instructions through their headphones.

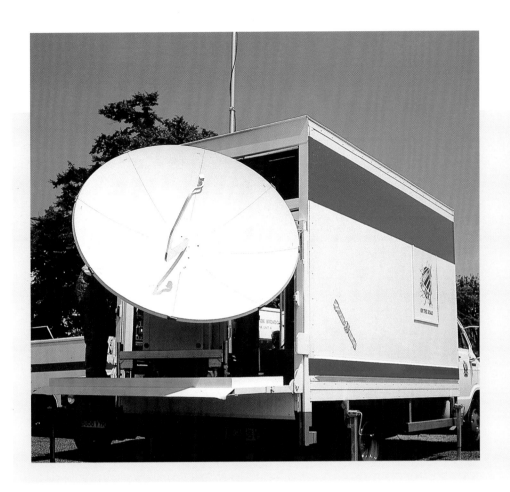

Outside broadcasts

News items and sports matches have to be filmed outside the television station. These are known as outside broadcasts. A mobile control room is used as the production control room. The pictures from the cameras are sent there before being relayed to the television station.

Left **This outside broadcast unit is carrying a folding satellite dish.**

Vision and sound control

The picture signals from the cameras are sent down a cable to the vision control room. Here, the pictures are checked by the lighting director for brightness, and by the vision controller for quality and colour.

Microphones in the studio pick up sound from the scene that is being filmed and convert it into electronic signals. These are sent down a cable to the sound control room. Sound engineers check the sound quality, and can change the volume and add music or special effects. The sound signals are then sent to the production control room, and checked alongside the picture signals by the director.

A video editor at work. If a programme is not going out live, it can be edited to make sure only the best parts are broadcast.

Transmission

TV signals

Television signals can be transmitted in either analogue or digital form. In an analogue signal, the information about how the sound and pictures are made up is transmitted in the form of electrical signals. In a digital signal, the sound and picture information is converted into a series of electronic digits. When the signal reaches the television set, the information is converted back into sounds and pictures by a decoder attached to the set. Sound and pictures transmitted digitally are of a better quality. Digital signals take up much less space than analogue signals, so many more channels can be transmitted.

In the early days of television, all programmes had to be broadcast live because the technology required to record them had not yet been developed. Today, most programmes are pre-recorded. This means that any mistakes can be taken out before the programme is broadcast. Programmes that are broadcast live are those where it is important to have the latest information, such as news programmes or sports matches.

Terrestrial broadcasting

The first stage in the process of getting television pictures to the viewers at home is called transmission. There are various ways in which this can be done. In terrestrial broadcasting, a transmitter at the television station combines the sound and picture signals of a programme and converts them into radio waves. The radio waves are sent out from the transmitting mast at the station to transmitters around the country. These relay the signals to the aerials on people's homes.

The 'forest of steel' near Albuquerque, New Mexico, USA. These are the highest television antennae in the world.

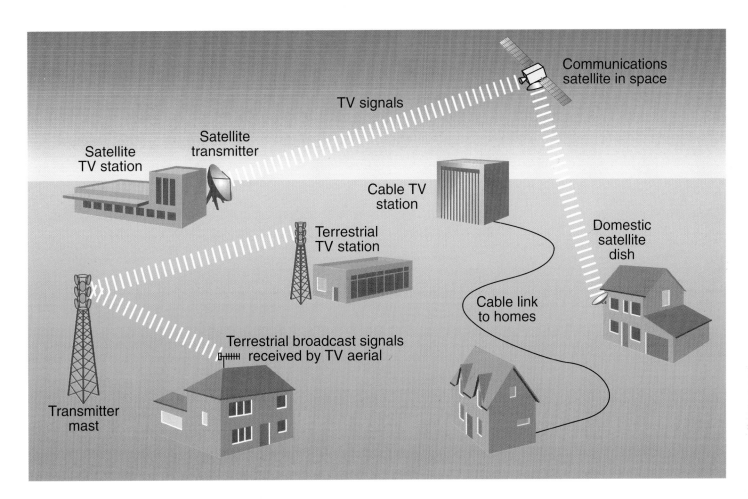

Communications satellite in space

TV signals

Satellite transmitter

Satellite TV station

Cable TV station

Domestic satellite dish

Terrestrial TV station

Cable link to homes

Terrestrial broadcast signals received by TV aerial

Transmitter mast

Transmission via satellite

The first programme to be transmitted by satellite was broadcast in 1962. Sent from the USA to Europe, it was received by 200 million viewers. Satellite transmission works by sending television signals in the form of microwaves into space from a large dish aerial. The signals bounce off orbiting satellites and are sent back down to earth. Here, they are picked up by another powerful aerial, which relays them to a network of local transmitters. Alternatively, the signals can be sent direct from the satellite to small satellite receivers on people's homes.

Cable television

Television signals can also be sent out through networks of underground cables. The signals are carried in the form of pulses of laser light, through optical-fibre cables. These are made of very fine threads of glass, and can carry dozens of channels at a time. Once the signals reach people's homes, they are decoded by a device on top of the television set.

Programmes can be transmitted using transmitter masts, satellites or cable links. Some homes are equipped to receive programmes by more than one transmission method.

Receiving programmes

Television signals reach viewers' homes via an aerial, satellite dish or cable. The signals travel along a wire into the television set. When the television is switched on, the sound and picture signals are separated. The sound is sent to the television's loudspeaker. The picture signal is sent to the cathode ray tube inside the set. Here, the signal is changed into the pictures that we see on the screen.

Making the picture

Inside the cathode ray tube, an electronic gun shoots the picture signals, in the form of beams of electricity, at the back of the screen. The screen is coated with a chemical that glows where the electric beams strike it. Each picture on screen is made up of hundreds of lines, which in turn are made up of thousands of dots. The electric beams scan back and forth across the screen sixty times per second. They strike the dots to make exactly the same pattern as the one picked up by the television camera when the programme was filmed.

A magnifying glass looking inside a cathode ray tube. The magnets make the electric beams scan across the back of the screen in lines.

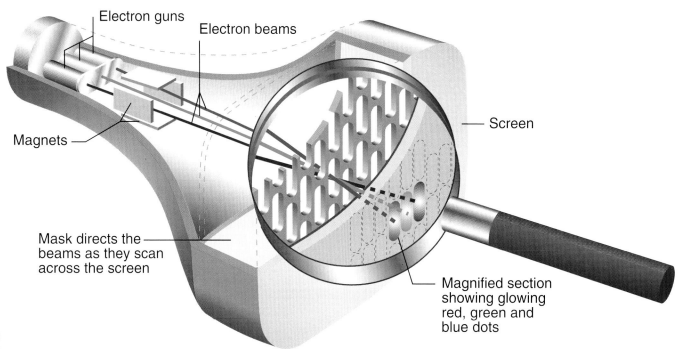

Electron guns

Electron beams

Magnets

Mask directs the beams as they scan across the screen

Screen

Magnified section showing glowing red, green and blue dots

A factory worker assembles televisions. The cathode ray tube can be seen in the centre of each set.

Choosing a channel

There are many television channels to choose from, each showing different sorts of programme. The radio waves that carry terrestrial and satellite television signals are divided into channels according to their wavelength and frequency. Each channel has room for only one station's signal. In cable television systems, the different channels are carried in the pulses of laser light in the optical fibres.

Remote controls

When you press a button on the remote control, you are sending a pulsing beam of infra-red light to a sensor inside the television set. The number of pulses will vary, depending on whether you want to adjust the volume or another control.

This viewer is using a handset to turn down the volume by remote control.

SPECIAL EFFECTS

By using special effects, film- and programme-makers are able to turn fantasy into reality before our eyes. Special effects have been around since the earliest days of film – they were used by innovative film-makers like Méliès, for example (see page 8). Sophisticated computer and film technology is used to produce special effects today, and this has had a tremendous impact upon what we are able to see on screen.

Computer worlds

With the help of a computer, images can be altered in many different ways – by being squashed, moved around the screen, or split, for example. Computer-generated images can even be used to create the world in which the action takes place.

Examples of computer imagery can be seen in action films such as *Twister*. In this film, the destructive tornadoes that provide the main storyline were created entirely on computer.

From the Producers of
"JURASSIC PARK"
and the Director of
"SPEED"

Don't breathe. Don't look back.

TWISTER

The Dark Side of Nature.

UNIVERSAL PICTURES and WARNER BROS. Present an AMBLIN ENTERTAINMENT Production a JAN DE BONT Film
HELEN HUNT BILL PAXTON "TWISTER" JAMI GERTZ and CARY ELWES Editor MICHAEL KAHN, A.C.E. Production JOSEPH NEMEC III
Director of Photography JACK N. GREEN, A.S.C. Music by MARK MANCINA Executive Producers STEVEN SPIELBERG, WALTER PARKES, LAURIE MacDONALD and GERALD R. MOLEN
Written by MICHAEL CRICHTON & ANNE-MARIE MARTIN Produced by KATHLEEN KENNEDY, IAN BRYCE and MICHAEL CRICHTON Directed by JAN DE BONT

A poster advertising the film *Twister*. The tornadoes look terrifying but they 'exist' only within the computer.

Chroma-key

One of the most useful forms of special effect is called chroma-key. Imagine, for example, that a programme-maker wants to show someone travelling on a flying carpet. The actor sits on a carpet laid out on a blue bench against a blue background in the studio, and pretends to fly. This is filmed, and the film is sent to the control room. Another film, showing the sky, is sent to a device called a switching board. Controls on the switching board direct the signals from the two films to combine together. Anything blue in the studio scene is made to disappear. This leaves a hole, into which film from the sky scene is inserted. The actor now appears to be flying on a magic carpet across the sky.

This technique can be used in many special-effects sequences. Weather forecasters can also do their reports in front of a blue screen – the map is added later, so the forecasters can only guess at what they are pointing.

A scene from the film *Con Air*. The helicopter is being filmed in front of a blue background. These shots will be combined with a sky scene later, so that the helicopter appears to be flying.

Animation

Animated films are probably the most popular form of film for children today. The films of Walt Disney, for example, have attracted huge audiences for many years. Animation can be achieved in a variety of ways, and some films even combine animation and live action.

Cel animation

The earliest form of animation was achieved by photographing a sequence of drawings, each of which was slightly different from the one before. This kind of animation is still used today. The process begins with a series of pencil drawings, which are transferred on to sheets of transparent film called cels. These are sent to the camera department, where each one is laid over the background scenery and photographed – frame by frame. When twenty-four frames of animation are shown per second in film form, the drawings appear to move.

A scene from the Walt Disney film *Pocahontas.* Walt Disney's animated films are very popular and have taken millions of dollars at the box office worldwide.

A scene from Nick Park's *The Wrong Trousers*. The film lasted approximately thirty minutes but took months of work to make.

Computer animation

New forms of animation include computer animation, as seen in films such as *Toy Story* and *Casper*. Images can be scanned into a computer or generated within the computer itself. Draco, the dragon seen in the film *Dragonheart,* started off as a wire-frame model, which was scanned into the computer. The dragon was then gradually built up using computer imagery and 'brought to life'. The images of the dragon were inserted into the scenes after filming had taken place. This means that, although on film the actors can be seen talking to Draco, they cannot actually see him.

Stop-motion animation

Stop-motion animation involves the filming of models or puppets. These are positioned and filmed for each shot before being moved ever so slightly and filmed again. When the shots are put together, they give the appearance of movement. One of the best-known model animators is Nick Park of Aardman Animation. He has won 'Oscars', the most important prizes in the film industry, for films starring the clay models Wallace and Grommit. Stop-motion animation involves a lot of time and effort. For the film *James and the Giant Peach*, only forty-five seconds of the movie were completed each week.

USING FILM AND TELEVISION

People visit the cinema for many different reasons – to escape from reality into a fantasy world for a few hours, to marvel at the special effects, or simply to enjoy a good story. When people are asked why they watch television, they often mention the need to relax and unwind at the end of the day. As well as being entertaining, film and television can also be very useful in our daily lives.

Bringing people together

The largest audience for a television programme so far was the audience for the opening ceremony of the Olympics in 1996. It has been estimated that 3.5 billion people watched this event. Television allows people to share the same experiences, although they may never meet. It can be a way of uniting the world and bringing people together on an occasion of joy or sadness.

A television camera films a tennis tournament. Television allows millions of people to share in the excitement of major sporting events.

WITH ALL THE BREATHLESS DRAMA AND SWEEPING ACTION THAT ONLY THE SCREEN CAN GIVE . . . . . .

NICHOLAS MONSARRAT'S BRILLIANT BEST SELLER COMES SURGING TO LIFE

JACK HAWKINS · DONALD SINDEN
DENHOLM ELLIOTT · VIRGINIA McKENNA
in

The Cruel Sea

PRINTED IN ENGLAND

Films such as *The Cruel Sea* told stories of wartime courage. They were designed to inspire the audiences of the 1940s and 1950s, who might one day be expected to show such courage themselves.

Spreading information

Film and television can be educational. News and current-affairs programmes, documentaries and natural-history programmes help people to find out more about the world around them. Many people enjoy watching films or television programmes set in the past, which can help them to understand why and how people in those times behaved as they did. However, it is important to remember that the producers present information in a way that is interesting or exciting for their audiences. This sometimes means that facts are left out, altered or made up, to create a better 'story'.

Propaganda

Before the age of television news, people used to visit the cinema to watch newsreels. During the First and Second World Wars, newsreels gave people vital information about how the wars were progressing. But the newsreels shown in Germany were very different from those shown in Allied countries. Each side would show its own version of events, emphasizing the successes and bravery of their own forces. The term for this is propaganda, and it describes the spreading of information that tries to persuade people to think in a certain way about an issue. Some governments today continue to use film and television as a way of spreading propaganda.

Market research

A viewer makes a note of the programme she is watching. The information she provides is used to help plan advertising and programme schedules.

All sorts of companies use film and television to advertise their products to a large audience. Many television companies make money by selling time on screen to advertisers who run commercials between programmes. Advertisers want to make sure that their commercials are being seen by the largest possible number of people. They also want to make sure that the people who are watching are those who are most likely to be interested in their products.

Checking the ratings

To find out how many people are watching the programmes on each channel, ratings companies are employed. They work in two ways. One way is to choose a sample of people who represent the whole population. They are sent diaries in which they write down every programme that they watch in a week. From this information, the total number of viewers for each programme can be estimated.

Another method is to install meters on television sets in homes across the country. The meter has a button for each person in the family to press every time they start and stop watching television. The meter records not only what is watched, but also the age and sex of the viewer.

Although the information gathered by ratings companies is used mainly by programme-makers and advertisers, it can also be useful in other ways. Sociologists, for example, would be interested in looking at the statistics, to see what they can learn about people's behaviour.

Programmes that appeal to children and teenagers are shown in the mornings at weekends.

Scheduling

Programmes are carefully scheduled to appeal to the audience that is likely to be watching at a particular time of day. Children's programmes are broadcast in the late afternoon, when the audience has come home from school. The biggest audiences watch in the evenings, when people are relaxing after a day at work. This is called 'prime time'. The programmes shown in prime time, such as game shows and soap operas, are designed to appeal to as many viewers as possible.

Television at work

Teletext

Certain stations broadcast a service called teletext. Viewers can obtain information by pressing numbers on their remote control. The information, which is put together on computer, appears in the form of text on the screen. The service is very useful for people wanting the very latest news – about the weather, sports results, business or travel.

Operation TV

Televisions and video cameras are used in hospitals during certain operations. To find out what is inside a person's stomach, for example, a surgeon inserts an instrument called an endoscope. The optical fibres in the instrument carry back an image of the inside of the stomach to the television screen, so that the surgeon can see what the problem is. An operation can be carried out using a laser beam carried by the endoscope.

Television screens are also used when pregnant women are given ultrasound scans – an image of the baby in the womb is transmitted to a screen and the hospital staff can check that the baby is developing properly.

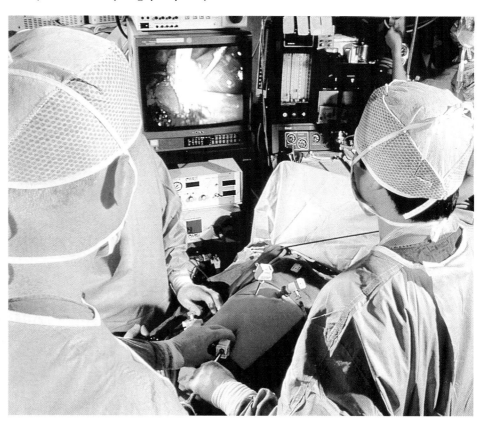

These surgeons are using an instrument containing a small camera to find out what is causing pain in the patient's stomach.

Left **Security officers keep an eye on what is happening outside the building by watching the screens. These display the images beamed in from video cameras.**

Below **Watch your speed! These roadside cameras photograph drivers who exceed the speed limit. The police can use the photographs as evidence.**

Television watchdogs

Security officers keep an eye on public places such as shopping centres, banks and railway stations, with the help of video cameras positioned around the buildings. The pictures taken by the cameras are monitored on screens at the control centre. If security officers see a crime taking place, they can send someone to deal with it quickly. The videotaped pictures can also be used as evidence in court.

Television in traffic

Video cameras can be used to help control traffic. Pictures from cameras positioned near busy junctions are sent to traffic controllers, who can programme traffic lights to help keep the traffic moving smoothly. If the camera pictures show that there has been an accident, or that some roads are very busy, the traffic controllers can warn drivers via travel news on the radio or electronic signs along the motorways.

THE FUTURE

All the developments described in this book have taken place in less than 100 years. So what about the next 100 years? How will television and film develop in the future?

The digital future

In the past, equipment such as telephones, televisions and computers all received signals and stored information in different formats – they could not 'communicate' with each other. Using digital technology, information can be converted into a series of electronic digits, which can be read by many different kinds of communications equipment. Home computers can be linked to telephone lines and the television.

Interactive television services will allow people to do their shopping without leaving home.

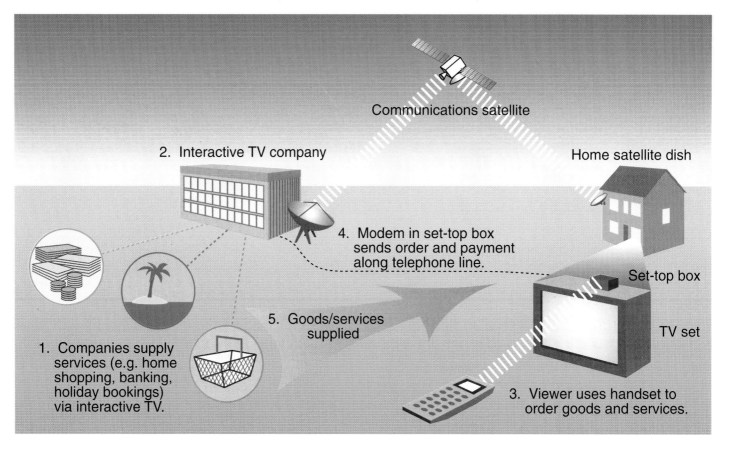

Communications satellite

2. Interactive TV company

Home satellite dish

4. Modem in set-top box sends order and payment along telephone line.

Set-top box

5. Goods/services supplied

TV set

1. Companies supply services (e.g. home shopping, banking, holiday bookings) via interactive TV.

3. Viewer uses handset to order goods and services.

Hanging your TV

Scientists in Britain are working on a new flat television screen that can be hung like a painting. When the television is switched off, the screen could display images, such as works of art. A television like this would save space in the home, as the screen would be hung on the wall. These new types of television could be ready for use in people's homes by 2000.

The same team of scientists is also developing screens that can be rolled up and carried around. This might be useful for soldiers, who could use the portable screens to display up-to-the-minute maps and information.

Left **A flat-screen television called the 'Plasmatron'. It is likely that we will all be watching televisions like this in the future.**

Soon, people will be able to key into events happening around the world by dialling up live videos. With the right equipment, it is already possible to make a phone call and see the person you are talking to on a screen. This facility is useful for people at work, who can take part in meetings without having to sit down together in the same room. It could also be useful for schools – pupils could take part in lessons, whilst sitting at home.

In the future, you will need just one machine for all of your communications. This will receive television programmes, and will have split-screens so that you can see more than one programme at once. Your machine will also act as a computer, accessing information from the Internet, and it will include a built-in video telephone.

Changing cinemas

A cinema audience enjoys the very latest in big-screen entertainment.

Once again, cinemas face a challenge from home entertainment. Since the 1980s, people have been able to watch videotapes of films at home. Today, they do not even need to visit a shop to rent or buy a video. Films are available on compact disc and can be downloaded from the Internet. People who own the equipment that is needed to select and watch the films can get a much wider choice, with higher-quality sound and pictures.

The big screen

Our visits to the cinema are also changing. IMAX cinemas show specially shot films on huge screens that are about 30 m across and 24 m high. Once the audience is seated, the screen fills their vision completely. The technique of 3–D cinema, first introduced in the 1950s, may make a comeback. More realistic 3–D images projected towards the audience will make people feel that they are sitting in the middle of the action. They will not have to wear the special glasses that were needed in the past to experience the 3–D effect (see page 11).

The emaginator

Emaginator rides add a new element to the cinema experience, and will soon be available in cities everywhere. People entering the cinema are strapped into their seats and made to feel that they are travelling on the journey seen on screen, as their seats move up and down or side to side very quickly. The trips offered by the emaginator include a ride on a rollercoaster, a trip down a mine shaft or a flight to the moon. Soon, we will not just be going to the cinema to watch a film, but to travel to places and dimensions never experienced before.

Step inside an emaginator and you may feel that you are actually experiencing the thrills of a rollercoaster ride.

Virtual reality

Virtual reality goes even further than 3–D cinema. A film leads the viewer through a series of events created by the film-makers, whereas virtual reality allows the user to interact with a computer-generated world. It is a bit like the difference between looking at a postcard and actually visiting the place. You can look at a postcard and wonder what the view would be like from a different point in the picture, but with virtual reality you can actually go and find out.

There are many ways of producing 'virtual reality'. Some use headsets, while others show a three-dimensional world on a flat computer screen. Many computer games use this system as it is a cheaper method than the headset system of producing a 3–D world.

The virtual-reality headset contains two TV screens providing stereo vision and headphones for stereo sound. The data glove and joy stick allow the player to fire a 'gun' at an opponent.

VRML

The computer language VRML (Virtual Reality Modelling Language) is used on the World Wide Web, which is part of the Internet. VRML allows three-dimensional worlds to be created, with which the users can interact.

In the USA, a computer network called Star Network allows children in hospitals around the country to interact with each other in virtual worlds generated by VRML. They can actually talk to each other and see a representation of the person to whom they are talking on the computer screen.

Virtual living

Film and television, together with other communications technology, offer us the opportunity to live in a completely new way. Soon, it will be possible for us to work, learn, shop, entertain ourselves and communicate worldwide from the comfort of our own homes. For many people, this is an exciting prospect – but it could mean never meeting another human being face to face again.

An optical-fibre cable. The hair-thin optical fibres are covered with plastic for protection. These small fibres of flexible glass represent the future of communications.

DATE CHART

1660s Magic lanterns are developed.

1830s The zoetrope is invented.

1888 The existence of electromagnetic waves is discovered by Heinrich Hertz.

1889 Celluloid film is invented by George Eastman.

1894 The Kinetoscope is invented by William Dickson.

1895 The Lumière brothers present the first public film show, in Paris.

1896 Electromagnetic waves are used by Guglielmo Marconi to send messages – the world's first radio broadcast.

1905 'Nickelodeons', the first cinemas, are built in the USA.

1907 The first 'Electric Palaces' are built in Britain.

1910 Hollywood begins to develop as a centre for film-making in the USA.

1925 John Logie Baird develops the first black-and-white television set.

1927 The first 'talkie' – *The Jazz Singer* – is released.

1966 Colour television is widely available.

1969 Around the world, 723 million viewers watch television pictures of the first man to walk on the moon.

1970 The first IMAX films are released.

1975 Video-recorders for use in the home are introduced.

1980s Multiplex cinemas are built and audiences increase.

1928 A television set is installed in a home in the USA for the first time.

1932 The first regular television programmes are broadcast from London by the BBC.

1941 The first television commercial is shown, in the USA.

1946 Sales of television sets boom after the Second World War. Stations begin broadcasting four or five times a week.

1950s Most cinema films are shown in colour.

1954 A colour television system is developed in the USA.

1956 Videotape recording is introduced to store programmes at television stations.

1960s Cinema-going declines as television takes over.

1990s The digital revolution begins, with access to the Internet becoming available to more and more people.

GLOSSARY

aerial The part of a television transmitter or receiver that sends or picks up signals.

animation The process of filming drawings or models one frame at a time, so that they appear to move when the film is run through a projector.

auditorium The area of a cinema or theatre where the audience sits.

blockbuster A film that costs a lot of money to make, looks spectacular and attracts large audiences.

commissionaire A person who greets visitors as they arrive at a cinema.

communications satellite A machine that orbits the Earth, receiving and passing on radio and TV signals.

control room A soundproofed room that overlooks the set in a television studio.

digits Numerals. Only 0 and 1 are used in TV signals, in many different combinations.

edited Rearranged or shortened.

electromagnetic spectrum The range of different electromagnetic waves. Light waves, radio waves and microwaves are part of the electromagnetic spectrum.

electromagnetic waves Invisible ripples of electric and magnetic force that travel through space.

frame A single shot on a strip of film.

frequency The number of radio waves that pass a given point in one second.

infra-red light A light that uses infra-red waves, which have a longer wavelength than normal light waves.

interactive television A system that allows viewers to communicate with the TV screen.

Internet The world's biggest computer network, which allows people all over the world to share information.

laser A device that produces a narrow beam of light.

microwave A type of electromagnetic wave.

modem A device that passes information from a computer along a telephone line.

optical fibres Thin threads of glass or plastic through which light travels.

photoelectric cell A device that produces electric current when it is exposed to light.

project To throw the images from a film on to a screen.

reception Picking up the signals from transmitters.

script The story that is told in a film or TV programme. It sets out the lines that the actors have to speak.

shutter The part of a camera or projector that opens to allow light to shine on to the film inside.

soundtrack The narrow band on one side of the film strip that contains all the sounds used in the film.

special effects Techniques used to create something that would be difficult or impossible to film in real life.

studio A soundproofed room where films or television programmes are produced.

takes Individual scenes, which may have to be filmed several times to make sure everything is just right.

3-D (three-dimensional) Appearing to have depth, so that on a film the action seems to come right up to the viewer.

transmission Sending out the electronic signals that carry television programmes.

usherette An assistant at a cinema who shows people to their seats.

wavelength The distance between the highest point of one radio wave and the next.

FIND OUT MORE

Books to read

The Digital Revolution by Stephen Hoare (Wayland, 1998)
Television by Christopher Griffin-Beale and Robyn Gee (Usborne, 1992)
Telecommunications by Chris Oxlade (Wayland, 1996)
The Young Oxford Book of Cinema by David Parkinson (Oxford University Press, 1996)
The Zigzag Book of Film and TV by Neil Cook and Kay Barnham (Zigzag, 1995)

Places to visit

British Film Institute (BFI), 21 Stephen Street, London
Provides information and publications about the film industry.

Museum of the Moving Image (MOMI), Waterloo, London
Contains many exhibits covering the history and development of film and television.

Film Education, Alhambra House, 27–31 Charing Cross Road, London WC2H 0AU
Provides free publications and information about the film industry.

The Science Museum, Exhibition Road, London
Displays a wide variety of exhibits including some relating to television.

National Museum of Film, Photography and Television, Prince's View, Bradford
Includes exhibits about the history of television, and a working television studio.

INDEX